fondue

A range of simple and delicious

recipes for all kinds of fondues

Lorraine Turner

p

This is a Parragon Publishing Book
First published in 2004

Parragon Publishing
Queen Street House
4 Queen Street
Bath BA1 1HE, UK

Copyright © Parragon 2004

Produced by The Bridgewater Book Company Ltd

Main photography by **Calvey Taylor-Haw**
Home economist **Ruth Pollock**

ISBN: 1-40543-794-4

Printed in China

Notes

• This book uses metric, imperial, and US
cup measurements. Follow the same units
of measurement throughout; do not mix
metric and imperial.

• All spoon measurements are level:
teaspoons are assumed to be 5 ml, and
tablespoons are assumed to be 15 ml.

• Unless otherwise stated, milk is assumed
to be whole, eggs and individual vegetables
such as potatoes are medium, and pepper is
freshly ground black pepper.

• Recipes using raw or very lightly cooked
eggs should be avoided by infants, the
elderly, pregnant women, convalescents,
and anyone suffering from an illness.

• Optional ingredients, variations, or
serving suggestions have not been included
in the calculations. The times given are an
approximate guide only.

contents

introduction

Derived from French—*fondre* means "melt"—fondues are creamy mixtures of cheese, white wine, and flavorings that originated in Switzerland. The ingredients are combined in the kitchen, then transferred to a ceramic fondue pot set over a burner. Chunks of bread are speared onto long-handled forks and dipped into the pot for a delicious and filling snack. Naturally, traditional fondues are based on Swiss cheeses, such as Gruyère, but modern recipes have introduced all sorts of other types, from fontina to Brie, with their distinctive characteristics. Additional flavorings range from the subtle to the pungent and include garlic, shallots, herbs, kirsch, brandy, and cayenne pepper. As this economical rustic dish has become more sophisticated and migrated from the countryside to the city, so the range of dippers has grown, and these days may include pita bread, garlic bread, olives, and raw or lightly cooked vegetables.

Fondues are suitable for a whole host of occasions, from simple, and very social, midweek family suppers to special dinner parties. They also make delicious and unusual dessert courses

4

Try seafood dippers for
a contemporary twist

Ensure meat is cooked
through in the oil or stock

Bread is the dipper-of-
choice for cheese fondues

Vegetables can be dipped
blanched or raw

Fruit dippers are perfect
for sweet fondues

The fondue bourguignonne is a later development. Oil is heated in a metal fondue pot, which is then set over a burner. It was originally designed for cooking pieces of steak, before dipping them in sauces and relishes and eating with pickles, mustard, and other condiments, but soon all sorts of delicious morsels were being be prepared in this way, from fish to tiny spring rolls. Marinating the dippers in advance makes them even tastier and an unusual treat is to coat them in a light batter before frying. Accompanying the fondue with a selection of salads and sauces balances the meal nicely.

The third kind of fondue derives from the Mongolian steamboat or firepot and is a popular dish throughout Asia. A variety of ingredients are speared onto forks and cooked in a stock in the pot. They may then be combined with other ingredients before being wrapped in Chinese leaves or lettuce pockets, or they may simply be eaten with tasty dipping sauces.

Finally, the dessert fondue was invented. The first choice is invariably chocolate, but toffee and syrup mixtures are also popular. Fresh fruits are easy dippers, but you can also choose cake, cookies, and fritters.

Enamelled cast iron fondue pots are very versatile, and are the best choice if you plan on cooking a variety of fondues

Stainless steel pots are good for meat fondues. Make sure it has a metal top ring to reduce the risk of being burned by spurts of oil

Earthenware pots are great for cheese and dessert fondues but they cannot stand the temperatures needed for meat fondues

vegetarian &
cheese fondues

The vegetarian fondues in this chapter are both nutritious and delicious—check out the Scallion & Leek with Tofu fondue (see page 28) or the Ravioli with Red Wine Stock (see page 26). For a taste of the east, try Mixed Vegetable Tempura (see page 34) or Mini Spring Rolls (see page 32).

Cheese fondues make delicious, protein-rich meals, and wonderful conversation pieces for social occasions. You can ring the changes by experimenting with different cheeses. For example, many people know about the excellent melting qualities of Gruyère and Emmental cheeses, but why not try Italian fontina cheese (see page 14), or a goat cheese such as Montrachet (see page 24)?

GREEK CHEESE WITH OLIVES, PITA & BELL PEPPERS

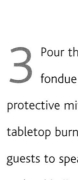

INGREDIENTS

1 large garlic clove, finely chopped
1 cup Greek dry white wine
14 oz/400 g Emmental cheese, grated
2¾ oz/75 g feta cheese
   (drained weight), crumbled
1½ tbsp cornstarch
2 tbsp ouzo
1 tbsp chopped fresh cilantro
salt and pepper

Dippers
whole dark kalamata olives, pitted
warmed garlic pita bread, cut into
   bite-size pieces
skinned red bell peppers (see page
   24), cut into bite-size pieces

1 Put the garlic and all but 2 tablespoons of the wine into a large pan and bring to a gentle simmer over low heat. Add a handful of the Emmental cheese and stir until melted. Add the remaining Emmental gradually, stirring constantly after each addition. Add the feta cheese and stir until melted.

2 In a bowl, mix the cornstarch with the ouzo, then stir into the pan. Continue to stir for 3–4 minutes, or until thickened and bubbling. Stir in the cilantro and add salt and pepper to taste.

3 Pour the mixture into a fondue pot and, using protective mitts, transfer to a lit tabletop burner. To serve, invite your guests to spear olives, pita bread, and red bell pepper onto fondue forks and dip them into the fondue.

EXOTIC MUSHROOM & HERBS WITH VEGETABLES

INGREDIENTS

2 tbsp butter

7 oz/200 g mixed exotic mushrooms,
   such as shiitake, chanterelle, and
   morel, coarsely sliced

salt and pepper

1 tbsp chopped fresh parsley

1 tbsp chopped fresh oregano

2 scallions, trimmed and
   finely chopped

³/₄ cup vegetable stock

3 tbsp lemon juice

³/₄ cup dry white wine

10½ oz/300 g fontina cheese, chopped

10½ oz/300 g Emmental cheese, grated

1 tbsp cornstarch

Dippers

fresh crusty bread, cut into
   bite-size pieces

selection of lightly cooked vegetables,
   cut into bite-size pieces

1 Melt the butter in a skillet over medium heat. Add the mushrooms and cook, stirring, for 3–4 minutes, or until tender. Season to taste with salt and pepper, then stir in the herbs. Remove from the heat.

2 Put the scallions into a flameproof fondue pot and pour in the stock, lemon juice, and all but 2 tablespoons of the wine. Transfer to the stove and bring to a gentle simmer over low heat. Add a handful of cheese and stir until thoroughly melted and bubbling gently. Repeat until all the cheese has been added and stir until melted. Stir in the mushroom mixture in small batches, until thoroughly incorporated.

3 In a bowl, mix the cornstarch with the remaining wine, then stir into the fondue. Continue to stir for 3–4 minutes, or until thickened and bubbling. Taste and adjust the seasoning if necessary. Using protective mitts, transfer the fondue pot to a lit tabletop burner. To serve, invite your guests to spear bread and vegetables onto fondue forks and dip them into the fondue.

GRUYERE WITH ASPARAGUS

INGREDIENTS
1 garlic clove, peeled and halved
generous 1¾ cups dry white wine
5 tbsp brandy
14 oz/400 g Gruyère cheese, grated
7 oz/200 g Emmental cheese, grated
3½ oz/100 g Parmesan cheese,
  grated
2 tbsp cornstarch
pinch of freshly grated nutmeg
salt and pepper

Dippers
fresh crusty bread, cut into
  bite-size pieces
small pieces of blanched asparagus

1 Rub the inside of a flameproof fondue pot with the garlic. Discard the garlic. Pour in the wine and 3 tablespoons of the brandy, then transfer to the stove and bring to a gentle simmer over low heat.

2 Add a handful of grated cheese and stir constantly until melted. Continue to add the cheese gradually, stirring constantly after each addition. Repeat until all the cheese has been added and stir until thoroughly melted and bubbling gently.

3 In a bowl, mix the cornstarch with the remaining brandy. Stir into the fondue and continue to stir for 3–4 minutes, or until thickened and bubbling. Stir in the nutmeg and season to taste.

4 Using protective mitts, transfer the fondue pot to a lit tabletop burner. To serve, invite your guests to spear pieces of bread and asparagus onto fondue forks and dip them into the fondue.

BASIL & FONTINA

INGREDIENTS
1¼ oz/35 g fresh basil,
    finely chopped
3 garlic cloves, finely chopped
10½ oz/300 g fontina cheese,
    chopped
9 oz/250 g ricotta cheese
1¾ oz/50 g Parmesan cheese, grated
2 tbsp lemon juice
generous 1½ cups vegetable stock
1 tbsp cornstarch
salt and pepper

Dippers
fresh Italian bread, such as
    ciabatta or focaccia, cut into
    bite-size pieces
selection of lightly cooked
    vegetables, cut into
    bite-size pieces

1 Put the basil and garlic into a large mixing bowl. Add all the cheeses and stir together well.

2 Put the lemon juice and all but 2 tablespoons of the stock into a large pan and bring to a gentle simmer over low heat. Add a small spoonful of the cheese mixture and stir constantly until melted. Continue to add the cheese mixture gradually, stirring constantly after each addition. Repeat until all the cheese mixture has been added and stir until thoroughly melted and bubbling gently. Mix the cornstarch with the remaining stock, then stir

into the pan. Continue to stir for 3–4 minutes, or until thickened and bubbling. Season to taste with salt and pepper.

3 Pour the mixture into a fondue pot and, using protective mitts, transfer to a lit tabletop burner. To serve, invite your guests to spear pieces of bread and vegetables onto fondue forks and dip them into the fondue.

FRENCH CHEESE WITH POTATO & BROCCOLI

INGREDIENTS

2 scallions, trimmed and chopped
2¼ cups dry white wine
12 oz/350 g Beaufort or Gruyère
    cheese, grated
12 oz/350 g Camembert cheese,
    rind removed, cut into small pieces
2 tbsp cornstarch
pinch of cayenne pepper
salt and pepper

Crispy potato skins
1 lb 10 oz/750 g medium potatoes
3 tbsp butter, melted
salt and pepper

Dippers
warm garlic bread or crusty French
    bread, cut into bite-size pieces
blanched broccoli florets

1 For the potato skins, preheat the oven to 400°F/200°C. Scrub the potatoes, pierce with a fork, and bake for 50 minutes. Let cool. Cut each lengthwise into 8 pieces. Scoop out most of the flesh, brush with butter, and season with salt and pepper. Arrange skin-side down on a cookie sheet. Bake for 12–15 minutes, or until crisp.

2 Put the scallions into a flameproof fondue pot with all but 2 tablespoons of the wine. Transfer to the stove and bring to a simmer over low heat. Add a handful of cheese and stir until melted. Repeat until all the cheese has been added.

3 In a bowl, mix the cornstarch with the remaining wine, stir into the fondue, and continue to stir for 3–4 minutes, or until thickened and bubbling. Stir in the cayenne and salt and pepper to taste. Using protective mitts, transfer the fondue pot to a lit tabletop burner. To serve, invite your guests to spear potato skins, bread, and broccoli onto fondue forks and dip them into the fondue.

THREE-CHEESE & BRANDY WITH CARAMELIZED ONIONS

INGREDIENTS

1 garlic clove, finely chopped
generous 1¾ cups dry white wine
9 oz/250 g sharp Cheddar cheese,
    grated
9 oz/250 g Monterey Jack cheese,
    grated
7 oz/200 g Brie, rind removed and cut
    into small pieces
1 tbsp cornstarch
2 tbsp brandy
salt and pepper

Caramelized onions
1 tbsp butter
1 tbsp olive oil
9 oz/250 g baby onions, peeled but
    left whole
1 tsp superfine sugar
1 tsp balsamic vinegar

Dippers
warm garlic bread, cut into
    bite-size pieces

1 For the caramelized onions, melt the butter and oil in a skillet over medium heat. Add the onions and cook, stirring, for 10 minutes. Sprinkle over the sugar and cook for 5 minutes. Stir in the vinegar and cook for an additional 5 minutes. Remove from the heat.

2 Put the garlic into a flameproof fondue pot and pour in the wine. Transfer to the stove and bring to a gentle simmer over low heat. Add a handful of cheese and stir until melted. Continue to add the cheese gradually, stirring constantly after each addition. Repeat until all the cheese has been added. Stir until thoroughly melted and bubbling gently.

3 In a bowl, mix the cornstarch with the brandy. Stir into the fondue and continue to stir for 3–4 minutes, or until thickened and bubbling. Season to taste with salt and pepper. Using protective mitts, transfer the fondue pot to a lit tabletop burner. To serve, invite your guests to spear the caramelized onions, garlic bread, and vegetables onto fondue forks and dip them into the fondue.

MUSHROOM WITH POTATO & GARLIC BREAD

INGREDIENTS

3 tbsp butter
3½ oz/100 g white mushrooms, diced
3½ oz/100 g cremini or portabello
    mushrooms, diced
salt and pepper
1 tbsp chopped fresh parsley
1 garlic clove, finely chopped

2 cups dry white wine
12 oz/350 g Brie, rind removed, cut into
    small pieces
12 oz/350 g Beaufort or Gruyère
    cheese, grated
2 tbsp cornstarch
2 tbsp brandy

Dippers
warm garlic bread, cut into
    bite-size pieces
baby new potatoes, steamed
small whole mushrooms,
    lightly sautéed

1 Melt the butter in a skillet over medium heat. Add the diced mushrooms and cook, stirring, for 3–4 minutes, or until tender. Season to taste with salt and pepper, then stir in the parsley. Remove from the heat and set aside.

2 Put the garlic into a flameproof fondue pot and pour in the wine. Transfer to the stove and bring to a gentle simmer over low heat. Add a handful of cheese and stir constantly until melted. Continue to add the cheese gradually, stirring constantly after each addition. Repeat until all the cheese has been added. Stir in the mushroom mixture in small batches, until thoroughly incorporated.

3 In a bowl, mix the cornstarch with the brandy. Stir into the fondue. Continue to stir for 3–4 minutes, or until thickened and bubbling. Taste and adjust the seasoning if necessary. Using protective mitts, transfer the fondue pot to a lit tabletop burner. To serve, invite your guests to spear garlic bread, potatoes, and mushrooms onto fondue forks and dip them into the fondue.

PINK CHAMPAGNE & CREAM

INGREDIENTS

1³/₄ cups pink champagne
10½ oz/300 g Gruyère cheese, grated
10½ oz/300 g Crottin de Chavignol
   cheese, or other goat cheese if
   unavailable, cut into small pieces
1 tbsp cornstarch
2 tbsp light cream
salt and pepper

Dippers
fresh crusty bread, cut into
   bite-size pieces
whole white seedless grapes

1 Pour the champagne into a flameproof fondue pot. Transfer to the stove and bring to a gentle simmer over low heat. Add a handful of Gruyère cheese and stir constantly until melted. Continue to add the Gruyère gradually, stirring constantly after each addition. Repeat until all the Gruyère has been added and stir until thoroughly melted and bubbling gently. Stir in the Crottin de Chavignol cheese until melted.

2 In a bowl, mix the cornstarch with the cream. Stir into the fondue and continue to stir for 3–4 minutes, or until thickened and bubbling. Season to taste with salt and pepper.

3 Using protective mitts, transfer the fondue pot to a lit tabletop burner. To serve, invite your guests to spear pieces of bread and grapes onto fondue forks and dip them into the fondue.

RED BELL PEPPER & GARLIC

INGREDIENTS

2 red bell peppers, cut into quarters
   and seeded
1 large garlic clove, finely chopped
generous 1 cup dry white wine
14 oz/400 g Gruyère cheese, grated
2¾ oz/75 g Montrachet cheese,
   or other goat cheese if unavailable,
   cut into small pieces
1 tbsp cornstarch
1 tbsp chopped fresh parsley
salt and pepper

Dippers
whole green and black olives, pitted
fresh crusty bread, cut into
   bite-size pieces
roasted zucchini, cut into
   bite-size pieces
red bell peppers, cut into
   bite-size pieces

1 To skin the bell peppers, flatten them and arrange skin-side up on a broiler rack lined with foil. Broil for 10–15 minutes, or until the skins are blackened. Transfer to a plastic bag, set aside for 15 minutes, then peel off the skins. Cut 6 pieces into chunks and reserve for dippers. Dice the remainder.

2 Put the garlic and all but 2 tablespoons of the wine into a pan and bring to a gentle simmer over low heat. Add a handful of the Gruyère cheese and stir until melted. Add the remaining Gruyère gradually, stirring constantly after each addition. Add the diced bell peppers, then stir in the Montrachet until melted.

3 In a bowl, mix the cornstarch with the remaining wine, add to the pan, and stir for 3–4 minutes, or until thickened and bubbling. Stir in the parsley and salt and pepper to taste. Pour into a fondue pot, and, using protective mitts, transfer to a lit tabletop burner. To serve, invite your guests to spear olives, bread, bell pepper chunks, and zucchini onto fondue forks and dip them into the fondue.

RAVIOLI WITH RED WINE STOCK

INGREDIENTS

Stock

1 garlic clove, chopped

2 onions, chopped

2 celery stalks

3 large carrots, peeled and chopped

1 quart water

1 bay leaf

3 fresh parsley sprigs

salt and pepper

3 tbsp red wine

Ravioli

1 lb/450 g durum wheat flour

4 eggs, beaten

2 tbsp olive oil

1 onion, finely chopped

4 tomatoes, peeled and finely
   chopped

3½ oz/100 g mushrooms,
   finely chopped

7 oz/200 g spinach leaves,
   blanched and finely chopped

1¾ oz/50 g Parmesan cheese, grated

2 tbsp chopped fresh basil

Dippers

selection of blanched vegetables,
   cut into bite-size pieces

1 For the ravioli, sift the flour in a mound onto a clean counter. Make a well in the center. Add the eggs and half the oil. Mix together well. Knead for 10 minutes. Set aside for 30 minutes. Halve, then roll out thinly into 2 rectangles. Cover with a damp dish towel.

2 In a skillet, cook the onion, tomatoes, and mushrooms in the remaining oil over medium heat for 8–10 minutes, or until the liquid has evaporated. Mix with the remaining ingredients. Place spoonfuls at intervals on one pasta rectangle. Cover with the other rectangle, cut into squares around the mounds, and seal. Cover.

3 Bring the stock ingredients to a boil in a pan. Reduce the heat and simmer for 1 hour. Strain into a heatproof bowl. Discard the solids. Pour into a flameproof fondue pot until two-thirds full, then bring to boiling point. Using protective mitts, transfer to a lit tabletop burner. To serve, invite your guests to spear the ravioli and vegetables onto fondue forks and dip into the stock until cooked.

SCALLION & LEEK WITH TOFU

INGREDIENTS

6 scallions, trimmed and chopped
1 leek, trimmed and sliced
2 celery stalks, chopped
3 large carrots, peeled and chopped
1 quart water
1 bouquet garni, made from fresh
   parsley, thyme, and rosemary sprigs,
   and a bay leaf
salt and pepper
1 garlic clove, peeled and halved
1 tbsp sherry

Dippers
7 oz/200 g firm tofu or bean curd,
   cut into bite-size pieces
selection of vegetables, such as
   broccoli florets and white
   mushrooms, and red bell peppers,
   cut into bite-size pieces

1 Put the scallions, leek, celery, carrots, and water into a large pan. Add the bouquet garni, season to taste with salt and pepper, and bring to a boil. Reduce the heat and simmer for 1 hour. Remove from the heat and strain through a strainer into a large heatproof bowl. Discard the solids and reserve the liquid. Arrange the dippers on a serving platter or individual plates ready for cooking.

2 Rub the inside of a flameproof fondue pot with the garlic. Discard the garlic. Pour in the reserved liquid until the fondue pot is two-thirds full, then transfer to the stove and bring to boiling point over medium heat. Stir in the sherry. Using protective mitts, transfer the fondue pot to a lit tabletop burner. To serve, invite your guests to spear the dippers onto fondue forks and dip them into the hot stock until cooked to their taste.

CRISPY EDAM MELTS

INGREDIENTS

scant 2 cups all-purpose flour
¼ tsp cayenne pepper
14 oz/400 g Edam cheese,
   rind removed and cut into
   bite-size cubes
1 tsp baking powder
1 tsp salt
2 large eggs

½ cup milk
4 cups peanut oil

Dippers
whole white mushrooms
whole cherry tomatoes
blanched broccoli florets
fresh mixed salad, to serve

1 Sift a generous 1 cup of the flour with the cayenne pepper into a large bowl. Add the cheese cubes and turn until coated. Shake off the excess flour, then arrange the cheese on a serving platter.

2 Put the remaining flour into a large bowl with the baking powder and salt, then gradually beat in the eggs, milk, and 1 tablespoon of the oil. Beat until the batter is smooth. Pour into a serving bowl.

3 Pour the remaining oil into a metal fondue pot (it should be no more than one-third full), then heat on the stove to 375°F/190°C, or until a cube of bread browns in 30 seconds. Using protective mitts, carefully transfer the fondue pot to a lit tabletop burner. To serve, invite your guests to spear the cheese cubes onto fondue forks, dip in the batter, and let the excess run off, then cook in the hot oil for 1 minute, or until golden and crisp. Cook the other dippers in the same way, or leave them without batter and cook to your taste. Drain off the excess oil and serve with a mixed salad.

MINI SPRING ROLLS

INGREDIENTS

2 tbsp chili oil

4 scallions, trimmed and
   finely chopped

1 red bell pepper, seeded and finely
   sliced into 2-inch/5-cm lengths

1 carrot, peeled and finely sliced into
   2-inch/5-cm lengths

3 oz/85 g bean sprouts

1 tbsp lemon juice

1 tsp soy sauce

salt and pepper

8 sheets phyllo pastry, halved

2 tbsp butter, melted

1 egg white, slightly beaten

4 cups peanut oil

Dippers

selection of vegetables, cut into
   bite-size pieces

To serve

1 quantity Asian Dipping Sauce
   (see page 38)

freshly cooked rice

1 Heat the chili oil in a wok or large skillet. Add the scallions, bell pepper, and carrot and stir-fry for 2 minutes. Add the bean sprouts, lemon juice, and soy sauce and stir-fry for 1 minute, then season to taste and remove from the heat.

2 Spread out the pastry on a clean counter and brush with melted butter. Spoon a little of the vegetable mixture onto one short end of each sheet of pastry, fold in the long sides, and roll up to enclose the filling. Brush the edges with egg white to seal.

3 Pour the peanut oil into a metal fondue pot (no more than one-third full). Heat on the stove to 375°F/190°C, or until a cube of bread browns in 30 seconds. Using protective mitts, transfer the fondue pot to a lit tabletop burner. To serve, invite your guests to spear the spring rolls and dippers onto fondue forks and dip into the hot oil until cooked (the spring rolls will need 2–3 minutes). Drain off the excess oil. Serve with the dipping sauce and rice.

MIXED VEGETABLE TEMPURA

INGREDIENTS

6 tbsp cornstarch
6 tbsp soy sauce
6 tbsp lemon juice
4 cups peanut oil
1 egg
1 cup ice water
1 cup all-purpose flour

Dippers
broccoli florets
white mushrooms
eggplant, cut into bite-size pieces
baby corn cobs, halved
snow peas
cherry tomatoes
freshly cooked noodles, to serve

1 Put the cornstarch into a bowl and turn all the vegetable dippers in it until coated. Shake off the excess cornstarch, then arrange them on a serving platter. In a serving bowl, make a dipping sauce by mixing together the soy sauce and lemon juice, then set aside.

2 Pour the oil into a metal fondue pot (it should be no more than one-third full), then heat on the stove to 375°F/190°C, or until a cube of bread browns in 30 seconds. Using protective mitts, carefully transfer the fondue pot to a lit tabletop burner.

3 In a separate serving bowl, beat the egg and water together, then stir in the flour briefly. Do not overbeat: the batter should be lumpy. To serve, invite your guests to spear the dippers onto fondue forks, dip them in the batter, and let the excess run off, then cook in the hot oil for 2–3 minutes, or until cooked to their taste. Drain off the excess oil, then serve with the dipping sauce and noodles.

AÏOLI

INGREDIENTS
3 large garlic cloves, finely chopped
2 egg yolks
1 cup extra virgin olive oil
1 tbsp lemon juice
1 tbsp lime juice
1 tbsp Dijon mustard
1 tbsp chopped fresh tarragon
salt and pepper
sprig of tarragon, to decorate

1 Ensure that the ingredients are all at room temperature. Put the garlic and the egg yolks into a food processor and process until well blended. With the motor running, pour in the oil teaspoon-by-teaspoon through the feeder tube until it starts to thicken, then pour in the remaining oil in a thin stream until a thick mayonnaise forms.

2 Add the lemon and lime juices, along with the mustard and tarragon, and season to taste with salt and pepper. Blend until smooth, then transfer to a non-metallic bowl. Decorate with a sprig of tarragon.

3 Cover with plastic wrap and refrigerate until needed.

ASIAN DIPPING SAUCE

INGREDIENTS

generous ⅓ cup rice wine vinegar

finely grated rind and juice of 1 lime

2 tbsp soy sauce

1¼ cups sugar

1 tbsp grated fresh gingerroot

1 tbsp grated fresh lemon grass

2 garlic cloves, crushed

1 fresh red chili, seeded and
    finely chopped

2 tbsp sherry

1 tbsp chopped fresh cilantro

1 Put the vinegar, lime rind and juice, soy sauce, and sugar into a small pan and place over medium heat. Stir in the gingerroot, lemon grass, garlic, and chili and bring to a boil, stirring constantly. Reduce the heat and simmer, stirring, for 5 minutes.

2 Stir in the sherry and cilantro, heat through for an additional minute, then remove from the heat and strain through a strainer into a heatproof non-metallic serving bowl.

3 Let cool to room temperature, then serve.

meat fondues

Beef, pork, and chicken are favorite meats for fondues.
For a special occasion the Sizzling Steak with Rich Tomato
Sauce (see page 56) is unbeatable, or try the ever-popular
Chili & Cilantro Pork Satay (see page 60). Oil fondues
offer an exciting and dramatic way to present food to your
guests. Remember to use a sturdy metal fondue pot and
place it securely, with its burner, on a heatproof surface
where it cannot be knocked over. Pat dry with paper towels
any marinated foods before immersing them in the hot oil,
otherwise they may splutter and splash your guests.

BLUE CHEESE WITH HAM-WRAPPED DIPPERS

INGREDIENTS
1 garlic clove, peeled and halved
generous 1¾ cups dry white wine
5 tbsp brandy
12 oz/350 g Gruyère cheese, grated
12 oz/350 g Gorgonzola cheese,
    crumbled
1 tbsp cornstarch
2 tbsp light cream
salt and pepper

Dippers
fresh crusty bread, cut into
    bite-size pieces
bite-size pieces of lightly cooked
    vegetables wrapped in cooked ham
    or strips of lightly cooked bacon

1 Rub the inside of a flameproof fondue pot with the garlic. Discard the garlic. Pour in the wine and 3 tablespoons of the brandy, then transfer to the stove and bring to a gentle simmer over low heat. Add a handful of cheese and stir constantly until melted. Continue to add the cheese gradually, stirring constantly after each addition, until all the cheese has been added. Stir until thoroughly melted and bubbling gently.

2 In a bowl, mix the cornstarch with the remaining brandy. Stir into the fondue and continue to stir for 3–4 minutes, or until thickened and bubbling. Stir in the cream and season to taste.

3 Using protective mitts, transfer the fondue pot to a lit tabletop burner. To serve, invite your guests to spear bread and ham-wrapped vegetables onto fondue forks and dip them into the fondue.

SMOKED CHEDDAR WITH HAM & APPLE

INGREDIENTS

2 tbsp lime juice

2 cups dry hard cider

1 lb 9 oz/700 g smoked Cheddar
    cheese, grated

2 tbsp cornstarch

pinch of ground allspice

salt and pepper

Dippers

4 apples, cored and cut into
    bite-size cubes, then brushed
    with lemon juice

fresh crusty bread, cut into
    bite-size cubes

canned pineapple chunks, drained

lean cooked ham, cut into
    bite-size cubes

1 Put the lime juice and all but 2 tablespoons of the hard cider into a large pan and bring to a gentle simmer over low heat. Add a handful of the cheese and stir until melted. Add the remaining cheese gradually, stirring constantly after each addition.

2 In a bowl, mix the cornstarch with the remaining hard cider, then stir into the pan. Continue to stir for 3–4 minutes, or until thickened and bubbling. Stir in the allspice and add salt and pepper to taste.

3 Pour the mixture into a fondue pot and, using protective mitts, transfer to a lit tabletop burner. To serve, invite your guests to spear pieces of apple, bread, pineapple, and ham onto fondue forks and dip them into the fondue.

ITALIAN CHEESE WITH MEAT DIPPERS

INGREDIENTS

1 garlic clove, peeled and halved

2 cups milk

3 tbsp brandy

10½ oz/300 g Gorgonzola cheese, crumbled

7 oz/200 g fontina cheese, chopped

7 oz/200 g mozzarella cheese, chopped

1 tbsp cornstarch

salt and pepper

Dippers

fresh Italian bread, cut into bite-size pieces

salami, cut into bite-size pieces

small pieces of apple, wrapped in prosciutto

morsels of roast chicken

1 Rub the inside of a flameproof fondue pot with the garlic. Discard the garlic. Pour in the milk and 1 tablespoon of the brandy, then transfer to the stove and bring to a gentle simmer over low heat.

Add a handful of cheese and stir constantly until melted. Continue to add the cheese gradually, stirring constantly after each addition. Repeat until all the cheese has been added and stir until thoroughly melted and bubbling gently.

2 In a bowl, mix the cornstarch with the remaining brandy. Stir into the fondue and continue to stir for 3–4 minutes, or until thickened and bubbling. Season to taste with salt and pepper.

3 Using protective mitts, transfer the fondue pot to a lit tabletop burner. To serve, invite your guests to spear pieces of bread, salami, prosciutto-wrapped apple, and chicken onto fondue forks and dip them into the fondue.

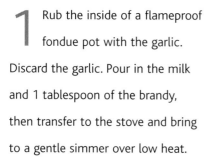

SPANISH MANCHEGO WITH CHORIZO & OLIVES

INGREDIENTS

1 garlic clove, peeled and halved
2 cups Spanish dry white wine
grated rind of 1 lemon or lime
1 lb 9 oz/700 g manchego cheese, grated
2 tbsp cornstarch
salt and pepper

Dippers
fresh crusty bread, cut into bite-size pieces
chorizo sausage, cut into bite-size pieces and lightly fried in olive oil
whole green and black olives, pitted

1 Rub the inside of a flameproof fondue pot with the garlic. Discard the garlic. Pour in the white wine and add the lemon rind, then transfer to the stove and bring to a gentle simmer over low heat.

2 Toss the cheese in the cornstarch, then gradually stir the cheese into the heated liquid, stirring constantly, until the cheese has melted and the liquid is gently bubbling. Stir until thick and creamy. Season to taste with salt and pepper.

3 Using protective mitts, transfer the fondue pot to a lit tabletop burner. To serve, invite your guests to spear bread, chorizo, and olives onto fondue forks and dip them into the fondue.

SHABU SHABU

INGREDIENTS

4 cups beef stock

5-inch/13-cm piece kombu (dried kelp), cut into small pieces and rinsed in cold water

5 tbsp soy sauce

6 tbsp lime juice

14 oz/400 g precooked udon noodles, or rice noodles if unavailable

Dippers

1 lb 12 oz/800 g beef sirloin, cut into thin, bite-size strips

7 oz/200 g firm tofu or bean curd, cut into bite-size pieces

8 scallions, trimmed and cut into bite-size pieces

1 Pour the stock into a large pan and add the kombu. Bring to a boil, then reduce the heat and simmer for 5 minutes. Meanwhile, mix the soy sauce and lime juice in a small heatproof bowl, then stir in 1 tablespoon of stock from the pan and set aside. Arrange the dippers on serving plates.

2 Pour the stock and kombu into a flameproof fondue pot (it should be no more than two-thirds full). Using protective mitts, transfer the fondue pot to a lit tabletop burner. To serve, invite your guests to spear the dippers onto fondue forks or place them on heatproof spoons, dip them into the hot stock until cooked to their taste (cook the beef right through), then dip them in the soy sauce mixture. When all the dippers are finished, add the noodles to the stock in the fondue pot and serve as a soup.

CHILI PORK WITH PEANUT SAUCE

INGREDIENTS

4 tbsp lime juice
3 tbsp chili oil
1 garlic clove, chopped
3 tbsp chopped fresh cilantro
1 lb 5 oz/600 g pork loin, cut into
   thin slices
4 scallions, trimmed and sliced
1 quart chicken or vegetable stock
1 tbsp grated fresh lemon grass
1/2 tsp chili powder
salt and pepper

Peanut sauce
generous 1 cup coconut milk
1 tsp red curry paste
4 tbsp smooth peanut butter
1 tsp grated fresh gingerroot

Dippers
7 oz/200 g firm tofu or bean curd,
   cut into bite-size pieces
selection of blanched vegetables,
   cut into bite-size pieces
freshly cooked noodles, to serve

1 Pour the lime juice into a large, shallow non-metallic dish. Add half of the oil, the garlic, cilantro, and pork. Turn the pork in the mixture, cover with plastic wrap, and refrigerate for 1 1/4 hours.

2 Heat the remaining oil in a large pan over medium heat. Add the scallions and cook, stirring, for 3 minutes. Add the stock, lemon grass, chili powder, and salt and pepper to taste. Bring to a boil, then reduce the heat and simmer for 25 minutes. Meanwhile, for the sauce, simmer the coconut milk in a separate pan for 15 minutes. Gradually stir in the remaining ingredients and simmer for 5 minutes. Drain the pork and thread onto wooden skewers.

3 Pour the stock mixture into a flameproof fondue pot (no more than two-thirds full). Using protective mitts, transfer to a lit tabletop burner. To serve, invite your guests to spear the dippers onto fondue forks and dip into the stock with the skewers until cooked (cook the pork right through). Serve with noodles and the sauce.

MARINATED BEEF WITH ASIAN DIPPING SAUCE

INGREDIENTS
6 tbsp soy sauce
5 tbsp dry sherry
1 garlic clove, chopped
1 tbsp grated fresh gingerroot
1 tsp sugar
1 lb 12 oz/800 g tenderloin steak,
   cut into thin, bite-size strips
4 cups peanut oil

Dippers
selection of vegetables, cut into
   bite-size pieces

To serve
1 quantity Asian Dipping Sauce
   (see page 38)
freshly cooked noodles

1 Put the soy sauce, sherry, garlic, gingerroot, and sugar into a large, shallow dish and mix together. Add the strips of steak and turn them in the mixture. Cover with plastic wrap and refrigerate for 1¼ hours.

2 Drain the steak, pat dry with paper towels, and thread onto wooden skewers, leaving space at either end. Arrange the skewers on serving plates with the other dippers.

3 Pour the oil into a metal fondue pot (it should be no more than one-third full), then heat on the stove to 375°F/190°C, or until a cube of bread browns in 30 seconds. Using protective mitts, carefully transfer the fondue pot to a lit tabletop burner.

4 To serve, invite your guests to spear the dippers onto fondue forks and dip them into the hot oil with the beef skewers until cooked to their taste (cook the beef right through). Drain off the excess oil, then serve with the dipping sauce and noodles.

SIZZLING STEAK WITH RICH TOMATO SAUCE

INGREDIENTS
1 lb 12 oz/800 g tenderloin steak,
    cut into ¾-inch/2-cm cubes
4 cups peanut oil
salt and pepper

Rich tomato sauce
1 tbsp olive oil
1 garlic clove, finely chopped
1 onion, finely chopped
14 oz/400 g canned chopped
    tomatoes
1 tbsp tomato paste
2 tbsp red wine
1 tbsp chopped fresh parsley
1 tbsp chopped fresh oregano

Dippers
baby onions, peeled but left whole
white mushrooms
cherry tomatoes
crusty French bread, to serve

1 For the tomato sauce, heat the olive oil in a small pan over medium heat, add the garlic and onion, and cook, stirring, for 3 minutes, until softened. Stir in the tomatoes, tomato paste, and wine. Bring to a boil, then reduce the heat and simmer gently, stirring occasionally, for about 25 minutes. Remove from the heat, stir in the parsley and oregano, and set aside. Arrange the cubes of steak and the other dippers on serving plates.

2 Pour the peanut oil into a metal fondue pot (it should be no more than one-third full), then heat on the stove to 375°F/190°C, or until a cube of bread browns in 30 seconds. Using protective mitts, carefully transfer the fondue pot to a lit tabletop burner.

3 To serve, invite your guests to spear the steak cubes and dippers onto fondue forks and dip them into the hot oil until cooked (cook the steak right through). Drain off the excess oil. Season to taste with salt and pepper. Serve with bread and the hot or cold sauce.

CRISPY-COATED PORK SAUSAGES

INGREDIENTS

1 lb/450 g pork bulk sausage
1 small onion, grated
6 tbsp grated Cheddar cheese
1 tbsp tomato paste
½ cup fresh bread crumbs
1 tsp turmeric
½ tsp paprika
salt and pepper
2 eggs, beaten
generous ¾ cup dried bread crumbs
4 cups peanut oil

Dippers
white mushrooms
eggplant, cut into bite-size pieces

To serve
1 quantity Mustard Dip (see page 68)
1 quantity Crispy Potato Skins
  (see page 16)
warm crusty bread

1 Put the bulk sausage into a large bowl with the onion, cheese, tomato paste, fresh bread crumbs, turmeric, and paprika and season to taste with salt and pepper. Mix together well and, using your hands, shape into small sausages about 2 inches/5 cm long. Turn them in the beaten egg, then coat them in dried bread crumbs. Arrange on a serving platter with the other dippers.

2 Pour the oil into a metal fondue pot (it should be no more than one-third full), then heat on the stove to 375°F/190°C, or until a cube of bread browns in 30 seconds. Using protective mitts, carefully transfer the fondue pot to a lit tabletop burner.

3 To serve, invite your guests to spear the pork sausages and other dippers onto fondue forks and dip into the hot oil until cooked to their taste (cook the sausages right through—they will need at least 3–4 minutes). Drain off the excess oil, then serve with the dip, bread, and Crispy Potato Skins.

CHILI & CILANTRO PORK SATAY

INGREDIENTS

2 tbsp lemon juice
3 tbsp vegetable oil
1 garlic clove, chopped
2 tbsp chopped fresh cilantro
1 tbsp grated fresh lemon grass
1 fresh red chili, seeded and
   finely chopped
1 lb 12 oz/800 g pork loin, cut into
   thin slices
4 cups peanut oil

salt and pepper
freshly cooked rice, to serve

Satay sauce
1 tsp chili oil
1 garlic clove, crushed
1 scallion, trimmed and finely chopped
1 fresh red chili, seeded and
   finely chopped
1 tsp Thai red curry paste

5 tbsp crunchy peanut butter
generous 1 cup coconut milk

Dippers
selection of fresh vegetables, cut into
   bite-size pieces

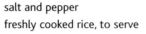

1 Pour the lemon juice into a large, shallow non-metallic dish. Add the vegetable oil, garlic, cilantro, lemon grass, chili, and pork. Turn the pork in the mixture, cover with plastic wrap, and refrigerate for 1¼ hours. Drain the pork, pat dry with paper towels, and arrange on a serving platter with the other dippers.

2 For the sauce, heat the chili oil in a small pan, add the garlic and scallion, and cook, stirring, for 3 minutes. Stir in the remaining ingredients, bring to a boil, then reduce the heat to a simmer.

3 Pour the peanut oil into a metal fondue pot (it should be no more than one-third full), then heat on the stove to 375°F/190°C, or until a cube of bread browns in 30 seconds. Using protective mitts, carefully transfer the fondue pot to a lit tabletop burner. To serve, invite your guests to spear the pork and dippers onto fondue forks and dip into the hot oil until cooked (cook the pork right through). Drain off the excess oil. Season, then serve with rice and the sauce.

SHERRIED ROAST CHICKEN

INGREDIENTS
4 cups chicken stock
generous ⅓ cup white wine
1 large garlic clove, chopped
1 tsp sugar
4 tbsp sherry

Dippers
1 lb 10 oz/750 g roast chicken breast,
    cut into bite-size pieces
2 red bell peppers, skinned (see page
    24) and cut into bite-size pieces
blanched broccoli and
    cauliflower florets
peeled carrots, blanched and cut into
    bite-size pieces

1 quantity Aïoli (see page 36),
    to serve

1 Pour the stock into a large pan and add the wine, garlic, and sugar. Bring to a boil, then reduce the heat and simmer for 10 minutes. Arrange the dippers on serving plates.

2 Stir the sherry into the stock, then pour the stock into a flameproof fondue pot (it should be no more than two-thirds full). Using protective mitts, transfer the fondue pot to a lit tabletop burner. To serve, invite your guests to spear the dippers onto fondue forks, dip them into the hot stock until cooked to their taste, then dip them into the Aïoli.

SPICY CHICKEN WITH BELL PEPPERS

INGREDIENTS

4 tbsp chili oil

1 tbsp lemon juice

2 garlic cloves, chopped

½ tsp paprika

½ tsp turmeric

6 skinless, boneless chicken
breasts, halved

salt and pepper

3½ cups chicken stock

generous ⅓ cup red wine

1 fresh red chili, seeded and
finely chopped

1 tbsp tomato paste

few drops of red food coloring
(optional)

1 tbsp cornstarch

Dippers

whole cherry tomatoes

whole black olives, pitted

1 red bell pepper, skinned (see page
24) and cut into bite-size pieces

1 orange bell pepper, skinned
(see page 24) and cut into
bite-size pieces

freshly cooked rice, to serve

1 Put the oil, lemon juice, and half of the garlic into a large, shallow non-metallic dish. Rub the chicken with the paprika and turmeric, then add to the oil mixture with salt and pepper to taste. Turn until coated. Cover with plastic wrap and refrigerate for 1¼ hours.

2 Pour the stock into a large pan and pour in all but 2 tablespoons of the wine. Add the chili, tomato paste, remaining garlic, and the food coloring, if using. Bring to a boil, then reduce the heat and simmer for 10 minutes. Drain the chicken, cut into thin, bite-size slices, and arrange on serving plates with the dippers.

3 In a bowl, mix the cornstarch with the remaining wine. Stir into the pan. Continue to stir for 3–4 minutes, or until thickened. Pour into a flameproof fondue pot (no more than two-thirds full). Using protective mitts, transfer to a lit tabletop burner. To serve, invite your guests to spear the dippers onto fondue forks and dip into the stock until cooked (cook the chicken right through). Serve with rice.

CHILI CHICKEN FIREPOT

INGREDIENTS

9 oz/250 g rice noodles
4 tbsp lemon juice
3 tbsp vegetable oil
1 fresh red chili, seeded and
   finely chopped
1 garlic clove, chopped
3 tbsp chopped fresh cilantro
6 skinless, boneless chicken breasts,
   cut into thin, bite-size slices
4 scallions, trimmed and sliced
1 quart chicken or vegetable stock
1 tbsp grated fresh lemon grass

½ tsp chili powder
salt and pepper

Dippers
selection of blanched vegetables,
   cut into bite-size pieces
whole cooked shelled shrimp
1 quantity Asian Dipping Sauce
   (see page 38), to serve

1 Put the noodles into a heatproof bowl, cover with boiling water, and soak for 4 minutes. Drain and set aside. Pour the lemon juice into a large, shallow non-metallic dish. Pour in half of the oil, then add the chili, garlic, cilantro, and chicken. Turn the chicken in the mixture (using heatproof spoons), cover with plastic wrap, and refrigerate for 1¼ hours.

2 Heat the remaining oil in a large pan over medium heat and cook the scallions, stirring, for 3 minutes. Add the remaining ingredients. Bring to a boil, then reduce the heat and simmer for 25 minutes. Drain the chicken. Arrange on serving plates with the dippers.

3 Pour the stock into a flameproof fondue pot (no more than two-thirds full). Using protective mitts, transfer to a lit tabletop burner. To serve, invite your guests to spear the dippers onto fondue forks, dip them into the hot stock until cooked (cook the chicken right through), then dip in the dipping sauce. When the dippers are finished, add the noodles to the stock and serve as a soup.

CHICKEN & BACON SKEWERS

INGREDIENTS

½ tsp turmeric
6 skinless, boneless chicken breasts
salt and pepper
4 cups peanut oil

Mustard dip
4 tbsp sour cream
4 tbsp mayonnaise
2 tbsp whole-grain mustard
1 tsp honey
1 scallion, trimmed and finely chopped
pinch of paprika

Dippers
4 lean unsmoked bacon slices
cherry tomatoes
whole baby onions, peeled
white mushrooms
sautéed new potatoes and a fresh
   mixed salad, to serve

1 Rub the turmeric over the chicken breasts, then season and cut into strips. Stretch the bacon slices until doubled in length and cut into thin strips lengthwise.

Roll up the slices of chicken and bacon and thread them onto wooden skewers with the other dippers, leaving plenty of space at either end. Skewer the tomatoes separately, because they will need less time time to cook. For the dip, mix all the ingredients in a bowl.

2 Pour the oil into a metal fondue pot (it should be no more than one-third full), then heat on the stove to 375°F/190°C, or until a cube of bread browns in 30 seconds. Using protective mitts, carefully transfer the fondue pot to a lit tabletop burner.

3 Invite your guests to dip the skewers into the fondue, and cook in the hot oil for 2–3 minutes, or until cooked (cook the chicken and bacon right through). Drain off the excess oil. Serve with sautéed potatoes, salad, and the dip.

seafood fondues

Fondues are a great way of serving fish and shellfish as the food is cooked quickly and so stays succulent and full of flavor. Some of the recipes use stock; these are sometimes known as "Chinese firepots," and are a wonderfully healthy way to cook food—infusing each morsel with exciting flavors. The Asian Firepot with Seafood Dippers (see page 76) is a great example. For a dish full of zing, nothing beats Romano & Chili Tuna Sizzlers (see page 78) served with a red chili dipping sauce. Light and fresh, fish fondues ensure that any party gets off to a sizzling start.

KOMBU & SEAFOOD

INGREDIENTS

5½ oz/150 g cellophane noodles
12 oz/350 g firm-fleshed fish fillets, such as cod, haddock, or angler fish, rinsed and cut into bite-size pieces
4 cups fish or vegetable stock

5-inch/13-cm piece kombu (dried kelp), cut into small pieces and rinsed in cold water
1 tbsp sake
6 tbsp soy sauce

Dippers
4 large peeled carrots, blanched and cut into bite-size pieces
1 lb/450 g raw shrimp, shelled and deveined
10½ oz/300 g sugar snap peas or snow peas, blanched

1 Put the noodles into a bowl, cover with cold water, and let soak for 30 minutes. Drain and cut into 3-inch/7.5-cm lengths. Meanwhile, bring a large pan of water to a boil, add the fish pieces, and cook briefly for 20 seconds. Drain, rinse under cold running water, and set aside.

2 Pour the stock into a large pan and add the kombu. Bring to a boil, then reduce the heat and simmer for 2 minutes. Pour in the sake. Arrange the fish on serving plates with the other dippers.

3 Pour the stock into a flameproof fondue pot (it should be no more than two-thirds full). Using protective mitts, transfer the fondue pot to a lit tabletop burner. To serve, invite your guests to spear the dippers onto fondue forks or place them on heatproof spoons, dip them into the hot stock until cooked to their taste, then dip them in the soy sauce. When all the dippers are finished, add the noodles to the stock and serve as a soup.

CREAMY SAFFRON SCALLOPS

INGREDIENTS

2 lb 4 oz/1 kg live mussels
2 tbsp butter
2 garlic cloves, chopped
4 scallions, trimmed and chopped
1 quart dry white wine

½ cup water
1 bay leaf
generous 1 cup light cream
½ tsp ground saffron or turmeric
salt and pepper

Dippers
7 oz/200 g raw shelled scallops
selection of blanched vegetables,
    cut into bite-size pieces

1 Soak the mussels in lightly salted water for 10 minutes, then scrub the shells under cold running water. Pull off any beards. Discard any mussels with broken shells or that refuse to close when tapped.

2 Melt the butter in a large pan over low heat. Add the garlic and scallions and cook, stirring, for 3 minutes. Add the wine, water, bay leaf, and mussels, bring to a boil, and cook over high heat for 4 minutes, until the mussels have opened. Discard any that remain closed. Strain the mussels, reserving the liquid, and shell. Discard the bay leaf. Arrange the mussels with the dippers on serving plates.

3 Pour the liquid into a flameproof fondue pot until two-thirds full. Transfer to the stove and bring to boiling point over medium heat. Stir in the cream, saffron, and salt and pepper to taste. Using protective mitts, transfer the fondue pot to a lit tabletop burner. To serve, invite your guests to spear the dippers onto fondue forks and dip them into the hot fondue for 3–4 minutes, or until cooked.

ASIAN FIREPOT WITH SEAFOOD DIPPERS

INGREDIENTS

9 oz/250 g fine egg noodles
6½ cups fish or vegetable stock
2 garlic cloves, chopped
2 shallots, chopped
1 tbsp grated fresh gingerroot
1 tbsp grated fresh lemon grass
salt and pepper
1 tbsp rice wine or sherry

Dippers
10½ oz/300 g raw shrimp,
   shelled and deveined
7 oz/200 g raw shelled scallops
10½ oz/300 g sugar snap peas or
   snow peas, blanched
baby onions, peeled but left whole
1 quantity Asian Dipping Sauce
   (see page 38), to serve

1 Put the noodles into a heatproof bowl, cover with boiling water, and leave to soak for 4 minutes, then drain and set aside. Pour the stock into a large pan and add the garlic, shallots, gingerroot, lemon grass, and salt and pepper to taste. Bring to a boil, then reduce the heat and simmer for 15 minutes. Arrange the dippers on serving plates.

2 Stir the rice wine into the stock, then pour into a flameproof fondue pot (it should be no more than two-thirds full). Using protective mitts, transfer the fondue pot to a lit tabletop burner. To serve, invite your guests to spear the dippers onto fondue forks, dip them into the hot stock until cooked to their taste, then dip them in the dipping sauce. When all the dippers are finished, add the noodles to the stock and serve as a soup.

ROMANO & CHILI TUNA SIZZLERS

INGREDIENTS

2 tbsp grated romano cheese
2 eggs
5 tbsp all-purpose flour
6 oz/175 g canned tuna, flaked
1 tbsp grated fresh gingerroot
1 tbsp grated lemon rind
1 cup corn
1/2 tsp finely chopped fresh red chili
4 cups peanut oil
fresh mixed salad, to serve

Red chili dipping sauce

1/2 cup plain yogurt
4 tbsp mayonnaise
1 fresh red chili, seeded and
　finely chopped
1 tbsp lime juice

Dippers

selection of vegetables, cut into
　bite-size pieces
whole cooked shelled shrimp

1 Put the cheese, eggs, and flour into a large bowl and beat together. Add the tuna, gingerroot, lemon rind, corn, and the 1/2 teaspoon of chopped red chili and stir together well. Meanwhile, for the sauce, put all the ingredients into a non-metallic serving bowl, mix together, and set aside. Arrange the dippers on serving plates.

2 Pour the oil into a metal fondue pot (it should be no more than one-third full), then heat on the stove to 375°F/190°C, or until a cube of bread browns in 30 seconds. Using protective mitts, carefully transfer the fondue pot to a lit tabletop burner. To serve, invite your guests to spear the dippers onto fondue forks and cook them with spoonfuls of the tuna mixture in the hot oil for 3 minutes, or until cooked to their taste. Drain off the excess oil, then serve with the dipping sauce and a mixed salad.

LIME & CHILI CRAB BALLS

INGREDIENTS

1 lb/450 g frozen crabmeat, thawed
2 tbsp freshly grated lime rind
1 fresh red chili, seeded and
   finely chopped
1 tbsp finely chopped scallion
1 tbsp grated fresh gingerroot
1 tbsp grated fresh coconut
2 egg yolks
4 tsp cornstarch

4 tbsp thick plain yogurt
2 tbsp sherry
salt and pepper
4 cups peanut oil

Dippers
7 oz/200 g firm tofu or bean curd,
   cut into bite-size pieces
selection of vegetables, cut into
   bite-size pieces

To serve
1 quantity Asian Dipping Sauce
   (see page 38)
freshly cooked rice

1 Put the crabmeat, lime rind, chili, scallion, gingerroot, coconut, and egg yolk into a bowl and mix together well. Mix the cornstarch with the yogurt and sherry in a small pan, place over low heat, and stir until thickened. Remove from the heat, mix into the bowl with the crabmeat mixture, and season to taste with salt and pepper. Pull off pieces of the mixture and shape into 1-inch/2.5-cm balls. Cover with plastic wrap and chill for at least 1 hour. Arrange the other dippers on serving plates.

2 Pour the oil into a metal fondue pot (it should be no more than one-third full), then heat on the stove to 375°F/190°C, or until a cube of bread browns in 30 seconds. Using protective mitts, carefully transfer the fondue pot to a lit tabletop burner. To serve, invite your guests to spear the dippers onto fondue forks (place the crab balls on spoons if not firm enough to spear), then cook in the hot oil for about 2–3 minutes, or until cooked to their taste. Drain off the excess oil, then serve with the dipping sauce and rice.

dessert fondues

There is no better way to round off a meal than with a luxuriously indulgent sweet fondue. Chocolate lovers will adore the Brandy Chocolate with Fruit Dippers (see page 88) and the Mocha with Amaretti (see page 94), while Nutty Butterscotch with Popcorn (see page 84) will prove irresistible to children and adults alike. For those of you who would like to add an extra sizzle to your meal's finale, the Chocolate Won Tons with Maple Sauce (see page 90) will capture everyone's imagination and have the whole household clamoring for more.

NUTTY BUTTERSCOTCH WITH POPCORN

INGREDIENTS

1³/₄ cups brown sugar
¹/₂ cup water
1 tbsp rum
6 tbsp unsalted butter
¹/₂ cup heavy cream, gently warmed
generous ¹/₂ cup peanuts, chopped

Dippers
popcorn
firm ripe bananas, cut into
    bite-size pieces
sliced apples

1 Arrange the dippers decoratively on a serving platter or individual serving plates and set aside.

2 Put the sugar and water into a heavy-based pan, place over medium heat, and stir until the sugar has dissolved. Bring to a boil, then let bubble for 6–7 minutes. Stir in the rum and cook for an additional minute.

3 Using protective mitts, remove from the heat and carefully stir in the butter until melted. Gradually stir in the cream until the mixture is smooth. Finally, stir in the nuts.

4 Carefully pour the mixture into a warmed fondue pot, then transfer to a lit tabletop burner. To serve, invite your guests to spear the dippers onto fondue forks and dip them into the fondue.

CREAMY RUM WITH BANANA

INGREDIENTS

²/₃ cup superfine sugar
4 tbsp water
1¹/₂ cups heavy cream, gently warmed
3 tbsp rum

Dippers

plain sponge cake, cut into
    bite-size pieces
firm ripe bananas, cut into
    bite-size pieces
sliced apples

1 Arrange the dippers decoratively on a serving platter or individual serving plates and set aside.

2 Put the sugar and water into a heavy-based pan, place over low heat, and stir until the sugar has dissolved. Bring to a boil, then let bubble for 3–4 minutes. Stir in the warmed cream and continue to stir for 4–5 minutes, or until smooth and well combined. Stir in the rum and cook for an additional minute. Remove from the heat and carefully pour the mixture into a warmed fondue pot.

3 Using protective mitts, transfer the fondue pot to a lit tabletop burner. To serve, invite your guests to spear the dippers onto fondue forks and dip them into the fondue.

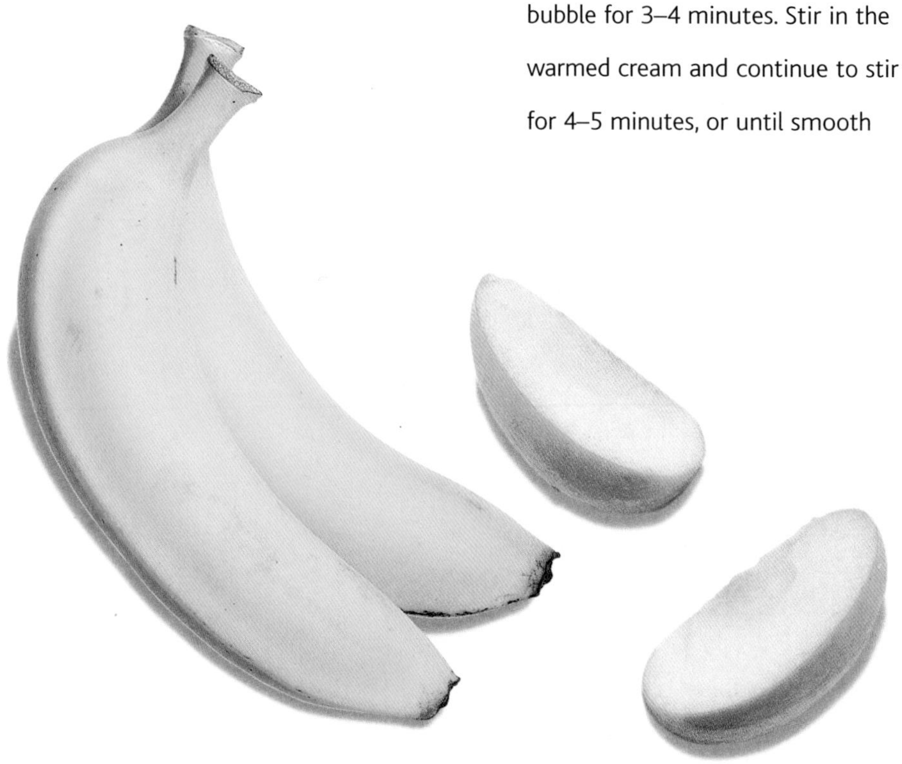

BRANDY CHOCOLATE WITH FRUIT DIPPERS

INGREDIENTS

9 oz/250 g bittersweet or unsweetened
    chocolate (must contain at least
    50 percent cocoa solids)
scant ½ cup heavy cream
2 tbsp brandy

Dippers
plain sponge cake, cut into
    bite-size pieces
small pink and white marshmallows
small firm whole fresh fruits, such
    as black currants, blueberries,
    cherries, and strawberries
whole no-soak dried apricots
candied citrus peel,
    cut decoratively into
    strips or bite-size pieces

1 Arrange the dippers decoratively on a serving platter or individual serving plates and set aside.

2 Break or chop the bittersweet chocolate into small pieces and place in the top of a double boiler or into a heatproof bowl set over a pan of simmering water. Pour in the heavy cream and

stir until melted and smooth. Stir in the brandy, then carefully pour the mixture into a warmed fondue pot.

3 Using protective mitts, transfer the fondue pot to a lit tabletop burner. To serve, invite your guests to spear the dippers onto fondue forks and dip them into the fondue.

CHOCOLATE WON TONS WITH MAPLE SAUCE

INGREDIENTS

16 won ton skins
12 oz/350 g semisweet
   chocolate, chopped
1 tbsp cornstarch
3 tbsp cold water
4 cups peanut oil

Maple sauce
³/₄ cup maple syrup
4 tbsp butter
¹/₂ tsp ground allspice
vanilla ice cream, to serve

1 Spread out the won ton skins on a clean counter, then spoon a little chocolate into the center of each. In a small bowl, mix together the cornstarch and water until smooth. Brush the edges of the skins with the mixture, then wrap into triangles, squares, or bundles and seal the edges. Arrange on a serving platter.

2 Put all the sauce ingredients into a pan and stir over medium heat. Bring to a boil, then reduce the heat and simmer for 3 minutes.

3 Meanwhile, pour the oil into a metal fondue pot (it should be no more than one-third full), then heat on the stove to 375°F/190°C, or until a cube of bread browns in 30 seconds. Using protective mitts, carefully transfer the fondue pot to a lit tabletop burner.

4 To serve, invite your guests to place the won tons onto metal spoons and dip them into the hot oil until cooked to their taste (they will need about 2–3 minutes). Drain off the excess oil, then serve the won tons with vanilla ice cream and the sauce.

VANILLA TOFFEE

INGREDIENTS

4½ oz/125 g butter
2 cups brown sugar
1 cup corn syrup
2 tbsp maple syrup
2 tbsp water
1¾ cups canned condensed milk
1 tsp vanilla extract
½ tsp ground cinnamon
1 tbsp rum

Dippers
cookies
firm ripe bananas, cut into
  bite-size pieces
sliced apples
bite-size pieces of chocolate
miniature cakes
shelled nuts, such as pecans or Brazil
  nuts, and walnut halves

1 Arrange the dippers decoratively on a serving platter or individual serving plates and set aside.

2 Put the butter into a heatproof bowl set over a pan of simmering water and melt gently. Add the sugar, corn syrup, maple syrup, water, condensed milk, vanilla extract, and cinnamon. Stir until thickened and smooth, then stir in the rum and cook for an additional minute. Remove from the heat and carefully pour the mixture into a warmed fondue pot.

3 Using protective mitts, transfer the fondue pot to a lit tabletop burner. To serve, invite your guests to spear the dippers onto fondue forks and dip them into the fondue.

MOCHA WITH AMARETTI

INGREDIENTS

9 oz/250 g bittersweet or unsweetened
    chocolate (must contain at least
    50 percent cocoa solids)
scant ½ cup heavy cream
1 tbsp instant coffee powder
3 tbsp coffee-flavored liqueur,
    such as Kahlúa

Dippers
cookies, such as amaretti
plain or coffee-flavored marbled
    cake or sponge cake, cut into
    bite-size pieces
whole seedless grapes
sliced firm peaches or nectarines

1 Arrange the dippers decoratively on a serving platter or individual serving plates and set aside.

2 Break or chop the chocolate into small pieces and place in the top of a double boiler or in a heatproof bowl set over a pan of simmering water. Add the cream and coffee powder and stir until melted and smooth. Stir in the liqueur, then carefully pour the mixture into a warmed fondue pot.

3 Using protective mitts, transfer the fondue pot to a lit tabletop burner. To serve, invite your guests to spear the dippers onto fondue forks and dip them into the fondue.

index